ANIMALS MIGRATING

HOW, WHEN, WHERE AND WHY ANIMALS MIGRATE

WRITTEN BY ETTA KANER

ILLUSTRATED BY PAT STEPHENS

Kids Can Press

Many thanks to Professor David Gibo from the Department of Zoology, University of Toronto, for his patience, time and interest in providing me with information and reviewing the manuscript. Thank you also to the wonderful team at Kids Can Press, especially my terrific editor, Stacey Roderick; gifted illustrator, Pat Stephens; and creative designer, Marie Bartholomew.

For Toby, Joel, Josh, Avi and Meira — the multiple migrations *mishpocha* — EK
For Katie — PS

Kids Can Press acknowledges the financial support of the Government of Ontario, through the Ontario Media Development Corporation's Ontario Book Initiative; the Ontario Arts Council; the Canada Council for the Arts; and the Government of Canada, through the BPIDP, for our publishing activity.

Published in Canada by
Kids Can Press Ltd.
29 Birch Avenue
Toronto, ON M4V 1E2

Published in the U.S. by
Kids Can Press Ltd.
2250 Military Road
Tonawanda, NY 14150

www.kidscanpress.com

Edited by Stacey Roderick
Designed by Marie Bartholomew
Printed and bound in China

The hardcover edition of this book is smyth sewn casebound.
The paperback edition of this book is limp sewn with a drawn-on cover.

CM 05 0 9 8 7 6 5 4 3 2 1
CM PA 05 0 9 8 7 6 5 4 3 2 1

National Library of Canada Cataloguing in Publication Data

Kaner, Etta
    Animals migrating : how, when, where and why animals migrate / written by Etta Kaner ; illustrated by Pat Stephens.

Includes index.
ISBN 1-55337-547-5 (bound). ISBN 1-55337-548-3 (pbk.)

1. Animal migration — Juvenile literature. I. Stephens, Pat II. Title.

QL754.K35 2005   j591.56'8   C2003-906537-5

Kids Can Press is a l'ORus™ Entertainment company

Contents

Introduction

Have you ever moved to a new home? If you were an animal and moved to a new home, you would have migrated. Why do animals migrate? Sometimes they migrate to a place where there is food for them and their young. They also migrate to set up their own territory and to mate. And sometimes animals migrate to a place where the temperature is cooler or warmer depending on what they need.

Animals migrate in many different ways. They might migrate short distances or long distances. They might migrate in groups or by themselves. They might migrate at night or during the day. Scientists used to think that animals migrated only when the seasons changed. This is true of some animals, like the gray whale. But many animals, like dragonfish, migrate every day. Scientists also thought migratory animals, or animals that migrate, always returned to their homes. But some animals, like army ants and locusts, just keep on moving.

In this book, you will find out all about animal migration. Move along with frogs and salamanders as they migrate to pools that disappear just a few months after they get there! Discover how hawks and eagles get a free ride when they migrate. And have you ever wondered how animals find their way or where they go? Just migrate through the pages of this book to find out!

Red-tailed hawk

Mammals

What do foxes, whales and zebras have in common? They are all mammals that migrate. Yet they each migrate in a very different way. Mammals may migrate back and forth, in one direction or even in a circle. They may migrate by themselves, like foxes, or in small groups, like gray whales. Some, like zebras and these Norway lemmings, migrate with thousands of others.

If you were a Norway lemming ...

- you would live near the top of a mountain.
- you would migrate short distances for food — between a dry place where lichens grow and a wet place where willows grow.
- you would migrate a long distance to another mountaintop when yours became overcrowded and you didn't have enough plants to eat.
- you and thousands of other lemmings would rush down the mountain to the valley below.
- you would jump into a river and swim across if the distance was short. If you survived the swim, you would make your way up another mountain to find a new home.

Follow that rain

If you know a big rainstorm is coming, you probably look for a dry place to stay until the storm is over. Wildebeests, zebras and Thompson's gazelles do just the opposite—they migrate in large groups toward the rain. They know that where there is rain, there will also be grass to eat.

These animals live in East Africa in the Serengeti National Park. Serengeti means "endless plains"—land that is flat, treeless and, depending on the time of the year, grassy. From December to March there is rain and plenty of grass in the southeastern part of the plains. But in June, after months of grazing by one and a half million wildebeests, zebras and gazelles and no more rain, the grass is gone. It's time to move on.

The huge herds thunder west and then north toward water and grass. They reach the full Mara River, where sweet grasses grow on the other side. The only way to get across is to plunge right in.

But many animals don't make it. Weaker ones are crushed by the crowd, carried away by the current or eaten by crocodiles. The animals that do make it eat their way across the northern part of the plains and then move southward with the rains and the freshly growing grass. By December they've gone full circle, and a few months later will follow the same route again.

Thompson's gazelles

Migration route

Mara River

Serengeti
National
Park

Wildebeests and zebras

9

Gray whales

Imagine living for three or four months without eating! That's what gray whales do while migrating from the Arctic to warmer waters to raise their young. How do they survive without eating for so long? They use their blubber, or body fat, for energy instead of food.

During the summer, before they migrate, gray whales build up a thick layer of oily blubber by eating a lot. They fill up on tonnes (tons) of tiny shrimplike animals called krill from the ocean floor. Early in October, when the days get shorter and the Arctic waters get colder, the whales start their 9600 km (6000 mile) trip south. Pregnant females travel alone or in twos or threes. Other whales travel in groups of about 12.

For the two months it takes to reach Mexico, the whales hardly eat. Even after arriving and giving birth, mother whales eat very little. They still depend on their blubber while they feed their babies milk.

After spending several months mating, giving birth and caring for their calves in warmer waters, the whales head back north to their summer feeding grounds. Both adults and young feed on the way since they no longer have a supply of blubber.

Gray whales

Migration route

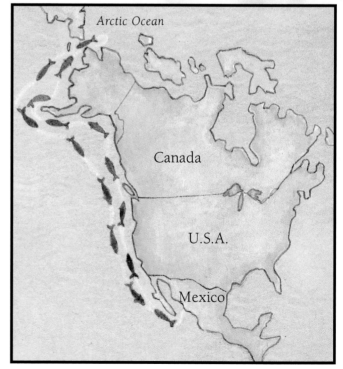

Arctic Ocean

Canada

U.S.A.

Mexico

Beautiful blubber

Whales depend on blubber for more than energy. Since they don't have thick fur, they need blubber to keep them warm. To find out how it works, try this activity.

You'll need:

25 ml (2 tbsp.) vegetable shortening at room temperature

2 sandwich bags

2 thermometers at the same room temperature

a freezer

1. Put the shortening into the bottom of one sandwich bag. Shape it into a ball.

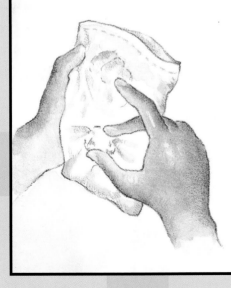

2. Push the bottom end of one thermometer into the middle of the ball.

3. Put the other thermometer into the empty sandwich bag.

4. Lay both thermometers in the freezer for 15 minutes. Then take them out and compare their temperatures. What do you notice?

The thermometer in the shortening shows a higher temperature because the shortening acts as an insulator. It slows down heat loss. Whale blubber does the same thing — it keeps the whales warm in the icy waters of the Arctic.

Leaving home

How old will you be when you move out of your family home? 19? 21? 25? Many mammals are only a few months old when they migrate to set up homes of their own.

A woodchuck leaves home when it is three months old. At first, it digs a burrow within its parents' territory. The mother woodchuck keeps her eye on her young one even though it's living on its own. She warns it with a sharp whistle when an enemy is nearby. Later the young woodchuck migrates again, this time to set up its own territory.

Red fox kits are born in early spring and leave home in autumn. Male kits leave first to avoid fights with their

Woodchuck

father. Females stay on a bit longer but will also leave their home range. Foxes may migrate up to 500 km (300 mi.) looking for a territory that is not already owned by another fox. When they find one, they spray urine on rocks, trees and snowbanks to mark the boundaries of their new territory.

Red fox kits

Young badgers also migrate from their family home in the fall. When females leave their mother, they usually stay in the same territory where they were born. But male badgers often leave the sett, or home, to find mates and set up their own territory.

Digging a new sett is a big job for a young badger. The badger moves tonnes (tons) of earth to form long tunnels. It gathers grasses and twigs for bedding.

And it even digs a shallow pit away from its sett for a toilet!

Black bear cubs are forced to migrate from their mothers when they're about two years old. When the mother is ready to mate again and raise a new family, she becomes angry and hits the cubs. Eventually they get the hint that it's time to leave. Each cub migrates by itself to set up its own territory.

Badger

Birds

At this very moment, birds somewhere in the world are migrating. Birds migrate short distances or long distances, like this Arctic tern. Some migrate during the day and some at night. Some fly over land and others over water. Some migrations take three weeks while others take more than three months. But birds are all migrating for the same reason — to find food for themselves or for themselves and their young. Birds that live where they have enough food don't need to migrate.

If you were an Arctic tern …

- you would be about 30 cm (12 in.) long and weigh as much as two small apples.
- you would live in a large group called a colony. Right before starting migration, the noisy colony would suddenly become quiet. Then the whole colony would take off.
- you would be the world's long-distance migrating champion by flying 35 000 km (22 000 mi.) from the Arctic to the Antarctic and back again.
- you would eat small fish, insects and shrimp on the way to keep up your strength.

Getting ready

Imagine flying nonstop for five days across the ocean! That's what the Pacific golden plover does. And it doesn't use an airplane — it uses its wings. Lots of birds fly incredible distances when migrating. How do they do this? Just as you pack a suitcase for a trip, migrating birds prepare for their trips, too.

For two or three weeks before migrating, the birds eat huge amounts of food. Most of this food turns into fat. Birds use the fat for energy during migration. Fat in a bird is like fuel in a car. The farther a bird migrates, the more fat it needs. Some birds, like the blackpoll warbler that flies all the way from New England to South America, almost double their weight in fat.

Birds also put on fat by changing their diet. Birds that usually eat insects, like the wood thrush, switch to berries and other fruit. This is because fruit turns into fat more easily than insects do.

But migrating birds need more than fat. They also need muscles. Their pectoral, or breast, muscles become larger before migration. These muscles help turn fat into energy and also power the birds' flapping wings.

As well as getting their bodies in shape, many birds that don't usually live in large groups gather in flocks for migrating. By joining a flock, a bird has a better chance of noticing and avoiding predators. And the bird can depend on others to find the right direction and to find food.

Blackpoll warbler

Pacific golden plover

It's not all smooth flying

Migration can be dangerous. Birds sometimes fly against very strong winds. They can suddenly fly into freezing air caused by a snowstorm. Or they can be confused by the lights on tall towers and fly into the buildings by mistake.

Wood thrush

Getting a lift

Some birds, like hawks, eagles, pelicans and storks, use very little energy when migrating. Instead of constantly flapping their wings, they use rising air currents called thermals to give them a free ride. Scientists call this soaring. To soar, birds spread their wings and tails wide and catch a thermal.

A thermal is a column of warm air that rises from the ground or water on a sunny day. A thermal can rise many thousands of feet into the sky, and soaring birds can rise with it. When a thermal cools and stops rising, birds pull their wings in a bit to move quickly down to the next thermal. By moving from one thermal to the next, a bird can fly several hundred kilometers (miles) a day using very little energy.

Swainson's hawk

Since thermals form over land more easily, soaring birds migrate over land as much as possible. When Swainson's hawks migrate from North America to South America, they follow the narrow band of land that joins the two continents. When eagles and storks migrate from Europe to Africa, they go out of their way to fly over the tiny country of Israel instead of over water.

White stork

Migration routes

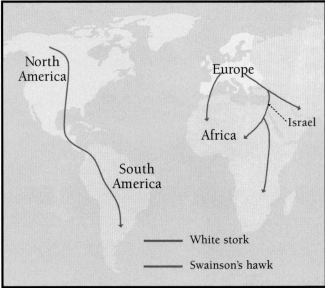

North America

Europe

Israel

Africa

South America

——— White stork

——— Swainson's hawk

Rising air

We can't see air. So how do we know that warm air rises?
Here's a way to prove it.

You'll need:

2 straight pins

2 paper
muffin cups

1 plastic drinking
straw

1 piece of thread
about 30 cm
(1 ft.) long

a light bulb in
a lamp that is
turned on

1. Stick a pin through the middle of each muffin cup. Push the pin through until the head catches.

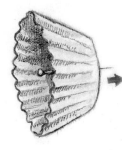

2. Stick the pins 1 cm (½ in.) in from each end of the straw. The muffin cups should hang freely.

3. Spread the sides of the muffin cups out a little bit.

4. Tie one end of the thread around the middle of the straw.

5. Hold up the other end of the thread and gently move it along the straw until the muffin cups balance.

6. With an adult's help, hold the thread so that one muffin paper is about 10 cm (4 in.) above the light bulb. What happens?

The light bulb heats the air above it. Since warm air is lighter than cold air, the air above the light bulb rises. The warm rising air, which acts like a thermal, is strong enough to push up the muffin cup. In the same way, warm air thermals are strong enough to allow large birds like hawks and storks to stay airborne without flapping their wings.

Finding the way

Landmarks

Just like you know the way to a friend's home by recognizing certain buildings, some birds find their way by following certain rivers, coastlines or mountain ranges. This is especially true of ducks and geese that migrate in families. The young birds learn the landmarks so they can use the same routes when they have their own families.

The sun

Birds that migrate during the day, like blackbirds, crows and blue jays, sometimes use the sun to help them find their way. For example, if they are flying south, they keep the sun on their left in the morning and on their right in the afternoon. Birds that migrate at night might use sunsets to help them find the right direction before they start.

Crows

Magnetic field

Earth is like a giant magnet. There are magnetic forces, or pulls, all around it. This magnetic field is strongest near the North and South poles. Scientists think many birds use these forces to help them find the right direction when migrating. The magnetic force feels stronger as the birds get closer to the poles. This cue can be used when the sky is cloudy.

The stars

Birds that migrate at night, like indigo buntings, sometimes use the stars to help them find their way. Scientists think birds use the patterns of the stars, as well as the North Star, to guide them.

Insects

Mammals and birds aren't the only animals that migrate. Insects migrate, too. Most insects migrate in one direction. They are looking for food and a place to lay their eggs. Insects that live for several months can migrate hundreds of kilometers (miles). Insects that live for just days or weeks, like aphids, migrate much shorter distances. Some insects, like army ants, migrate by walking in huge groups. Many insects, like this green darner dragonfly, migrate by flying.

If you were a migratory dragonfly ...

- you would be a strong and fast flier.
- you would migrate south before the weather turns too cold.
- you would return north to breed when the weather starts to warm up.
- you would find the way to your new home by following rivers, coastlines or mountain ranges.
- you would catch and eat flies and mosquitoes while migrating.
- you would migrate either long distances, like this common green darner, or short distances, like a meadowhawk dragonfly.

One-way trips

Picture this. You're hungry. You open the fridge to find it empty. You open the kitchen cupboards. No food. Instead of going to the store, you move to another house. In fact, you do this every time you run out of food. That's what life is like for many migrating insects.

Aphids may have to do this only once in their short lives. Aphids eat by sucking sap out of plants. When a plant becomes overcrowded, aphids migrate. They fly up into the air just above the treetops. Then they let the wind carry them along. As soon as they see a good feeding site, they fly down to it. The less time they spend up in the air, the better. They don't want to be a meal for a hungry bird.

Locusts also migrate in the air looking for food. Some, called solitary locusts, migrate at night on their own. Others, called swarming locusts, migrate during the day in groups of millions.

Amazingly, solitary locusts and swarming locusts start out the same. What they become all depends on how much food the hoppers, or young locusts, have as they grow up. If they have lots to eat and don't have to travel far, they become solitary locusts. If they don't have much food and have to hop across the country looking for more, they become swarming locusts.

Aphids

Locusts

Army ants migrate on the ground at night. The colony of millions moves in long, wide lines looking for food. As the ants march along, they eat everything in their way—insects, tarantulas, lizards, snakes and even birds!

Army ants

Butterflies and moths

You've probably heard about butterflies and moths migrating south in the fall and north in the spring. But did you know that the ones flying north are not necessarily the same ones that first flew south? They are the children and grandchildren of the first group. This is called remigration.

The most famous butterfly that remigrates is the monarch. In the fall, when the nights get longer and cooler, monarchs migrate south from North America to Mexico. After spending the winter in Mexico, they start to migrate north. On the way, they lay eggs and die. These eggs produce monarchs that fly back to North America in July or August. Then the cycle starts all over again.

Other butterflies, like the painted lady, also remigrate, but it's the grandchildren rather than the adults that start the trip back north.

Invasion of the migrating moths

Millions of migrating bogong moths invaded a stadium during the 2000 Olympic Games in southern Australia. Scientists believe the furry brown moths were confused by the bright lights of the stadium. The moths probably thought the lights were the moon, which they use to help guide them while migrating.

Painted lady butterfly

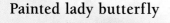

A sun compass

How do migrating butterflies and other insects know the right direction? They use the position of the sun and a sense of time to help them find their way. Find out how this works.

You'll need:

a watch or clock

a compass

a sheet of paper

a pencil

1. On a sunny day, go outside at 9:00 AM. Stand in an open place so you can see where the sun is in the sky.

2. Use the compass to find where south is, and stand facing it. Where is the sun? Is it on your left side or on your right side?

3. Do the same thing at 10:00 AM, 11:00 AM, 1:00 PM, 2:00 PM and 3:00 PM. Record where the sun is each time. When is it on your left? When is it on your right?

Scientists believe that when butterflies and other insects migrate south, they keep the sun on their left before noon and on their right after noon. When they migrate north, they do the opposite. How do they know how to change the angle of their body as the sun moves across the sky? Scientists are still trying to figure that out. What they do know is that all animals have a sense of time. This helps butterflies and insects use the position of the sun to help them find their way.

Sea life

It's amazing how many different kinds of animals use the sea when migrating —fish, crabs, worms and even tiny animals called zooplankton. Some of these animals, like spider crabs, migrate only when it's time to breed, or produce babies. Others, like zooplankton, migrate to find food. Many fish migrate for both reasons. Some, like this sockeye salmon, have a long and dangerous trip when they do so.

If you were a salmon ...

- you would start your life in a river eating worms and insects to grow bigger.
- you would migrate tail first to the sea when you were about 10 cm (4 in.) long.
- you would spend between four and eight years in the sea, migrating for food and growing into an adult.
- you would then work hard to migrate back to the place where you were born to mate and lay eggs. For this last migration of your life you would swim against the current, over rocks, up waterfalls and, hopefully, past fishers and hungry bears.

Fishy migrations

Just as a strong wind can push you down the street, water currents can push fish in the sea. This is useful for fish that migrate long distances.

The larvae, or young, of the European eel look like small curled-up leaves. They need to migrate all the way from the Sargasso Sea in the Caribbean to the lakes and rivers of Europe. Luckily, water currents in the Atlantic Ocean can carry them across. Still, it can take them up to three years to get there!

After spending from 6 to 20 years maturing in fresh water, European eels migrate back to the sea. On the way, they often need to wriggle over wet grass like snakes. But eels aren't snakes. They're fish! Their thick skins and narrow gill openings stop them from drying out.

Bluefin tuna are much bigger than baby European eels — about as long as two bathtubs laid end to end — but they also use the currents of the Atlantic when migrating for food. Rather than drifting, they swim with the current. This way, they use less energy when they move north in the summer and south in the fall.

European eel migration route

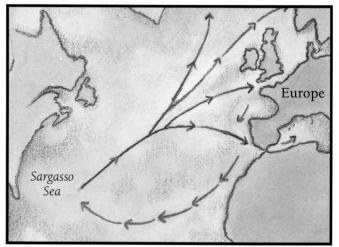

European eel

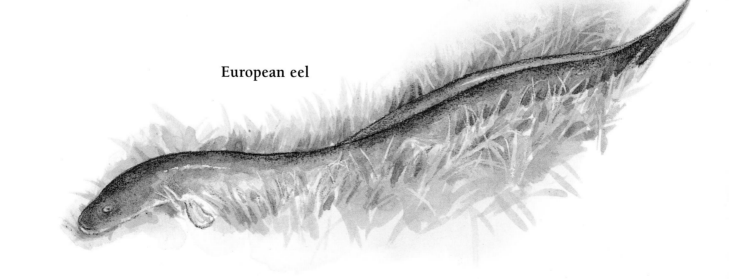

Watch out for crustaceans!

Some beaches are good places to see crustaceans, or animals with hard shells, migrate.

On Christmas Island in the Indian Ocean, the beach is covered with millions of red crabs in November. They migrate from their burrows in the hills to mate on the beach. After mating, the males return to the hills while the females wait for two weeks to lay their eggs in the sea. As soon as the eggs hit the water, they hatch. The females return to the hills while the young spend a month growing in the deep sea.

When the young crabs have grown as big as your baby fingernail, they also migrate up to the hills. Amazingly, the young find their way even though they've never been there before. Once again the whole island is covered in red — streets, houses, schools and even toilet bowls!

Spider crabs also migrate to beaches for mating, but they come from the ocean. So many crabs gather in early summer that there are huge piles of them on the shore. After mating, the crabs migrate back, carrying their eggs to deep water.

Red crabs

What goes up must come down

How are some sea creatures like elevators? They both go up and down. Every night, tiny animals called zooplankton swim up to the surface of the water to feed on microscopic plants. In the morning, they migrate back down into the ocean to try to avoid predators. Some larger sea creatures also follow this daily migration because zooplankton are their food. Dragonfish and krill live near the sea bottom during the day and swim up to feed on the zooplankton at night.

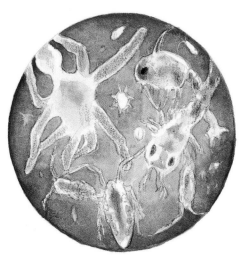

Magnified zooplankton

Dragonfish

A tale of a tail

Only one part of a palolo worm migrates — its tail. The tail migrates up to the surface of the ocean carrying the worm's eggs, where they hatch. In the meantime, the rest of the worm is busy in its burrow growing a new tail.

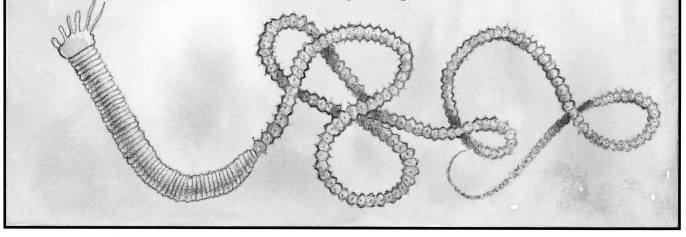

Moving up and down

How does a fish migrate up and down in the water?
Here's your chance to find out.

You'll need:

1 plastic sandwich bag

75 mL (⅓ cup) vinegar

2 clothespins

75 mL (⅓ cup) baking soda

1. Fill a kitchen sink three-quarters full of water.

2. Pour the vinegar into the sandwich bag. Twist the bag a few times right above the vinegar and hold it closed with a clothespin.

3. Pour the baking soda into the bag. Twist the top of the bag and close it with the other clothespin.

4. Put the bag in the sink. Remove the first clothespin and untwist the bag. What happens?

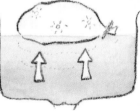

When the vinegar and soda mix, they form a gas called carbon dioxide. As the gas fills the bag, the bag rises to the surface of the water. The same thing happens with bony fish. Their bodies have a swim bladder that is filled with gas to keep the fish afloat. To swim up, the fish take in more gas from their blood. To swim down, they push out gas from the swim bladder.

Swim bladder

Reptiles and amphibians

Reptiles — like alligators, crocodiles and turtles — are born on land, migrate to water to mature and then migrate back to land to lay their eggs. Amphibians — like frogs, toads, salamanders and newts — are born in water, migrate to land to mature and migrate back to water to breed. Both reptiles and amphibians use water when migrating.

Most reptiles and amphibians don't migrate far. They migrate between feeding grounds and breeding grounds. Some amphibians, like this red-bellied newt, also migrate to hibernate.

If you were a red-bellied newt ...

- you would be born in the spring in a stream in northwestern California.
- you would migrate up a mountainside to hibernate underground during the dry summer, but come out to feed on plants during the autumn rains.
- you would migrate back to the same stream where you were born when it is time to breed.
- you would arrive at the stream in February if you were a male.
- you would arrive at the stream in March and April to lay eggs if you were a female.

Sea turtles

Imagine migrating to a new home right after you were born. That's what sea turtles do. As soon as they hatch from their eggs, they scurry down the beach to the sea. Amazingly, they always head in the right direction. How do they know where to go? Some scientists think they use the bright light of the ocean sky to guide them. Other scientists think that they have something like a magnetic compass inside their bodies that guides them away from the beach.

Sea turtle

Sea turtles spend their first 10 to 15 years maturing. When they are ready to mate, the turtles migrate hundreds of kilometers (miles) from their feeding grounds to the very beach where they were born! The females dig a nest in the sand with their flippers and lay their eggs in it. Leaving the eggs to hatch on their own, the females migrate all the way back to their feeding grounds in the ocean. Every few years, they return to the same beach to nest again.

Keeping track

How do scientists learn about a turtle's speed, location and distance as it migrates? They attach a transmitter to its back. The transmitter sends signals to a satellite that circles Earth. This is the same satellite that sends information about the weather. When the satellite gets a signal from the turtle's transmitter, the information goes to a computer on the ground.

Migrating with magnets

How do sea turtles find their way back to the beach where they were born? Some scientists think that sea turtles, birds and other animals use Earth's magnetic field to help them find their way during migration. Here's how it works.

You'll need:

a small piece of steel wool

scissors

2 pieces of clear tape, each 5 cm (2.5 in.) long

1 bar magnet

1. Cut off tiny pieces of steel wool and let them fall on the sticky side of one of the pieces of tape.

2. Cover the first piece of tape with the second piece, sticky side down.

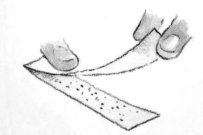

3. Hold one end of the bar magnet near the tape. What happens? What happens if you use the other end?

Scientists believe Earth is like a giant bar magnet and that it has a magnetic field. Scientists also think that, just like the steel wool bits are attracted to the bar magnet, migrating animals are attracted to Earth's magnetic field. This helps animals find their way when migrating over long distances.

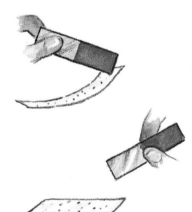

Earth's magnetic field

Here today, gone tomorrow

Many amphibians migrate to lay their eggs. But some frogs and salamanders migrate to breed in ponds that will disappear! These ponds are called vernal pools. They form in spring when rains fill large holes in the ground. By fall, they have usually dried up.

Every spring, hundreds of adult wood frogs migrate from woodlands to vernal pools. They migrate at night, during the first heavy downpour. After mating and laying jellylike masses of eggs, the frogs migrate back to the woods.

About three weeks later, the eggs hatch and the tadpoles start to grow quickly. Once the tadpoles have turned into frogs, they, too, make their way to the woods. This usually happens around the time the vernal pools dry up.

Mole salamanders — like spotted, Jefferson's and blue-spotted salamanders — also migrate to vernal pools to breed. They leave their underground homes during the first spring rains and can travel as far as 300 m (1000 ft.) to get to their breeding pool. This may not seem very far, but it is quite a distance for a 10 cm (4 in.) salamander. After several weeks of feeding and growing, the young salamanders migrate to the woods to find underground homes for the rest of the year.

Wood frogs

Amphibian crossing

For frogs and salamanders, migration can be a dangerous business. Every year, hundreds are run over on roads built through their territory. People try to help by building tunnels under the roads for the amphibians to use, by closing roads during migration season and by putting up signs like this one.

Blue-spotted salamander

Index